Vancouver

Vancouver

Featuring the photography of Duncan McDougall F.R.P.S.

Text by Peter Scholfield

Published by

Whitecap Books Ltd.,
2229 Jefferson Ave.,
West Vancouver, B.C.
V7V 2A9

First Printing 1978
Second Printing 1978
Third Printing 1979
Fourth (revised) Printing 1980

ISBN 0-920620-00-0 (Paperback)
ISBN 0-920620-01-9 (Hard Cover)
Printed in Canada

Other titles available in this series from Whitecap Books:—
Toronto, Manitoba, Shining Mountains, The Yukon, British Columbia, Victoria, Calgary, Edmonton.

in preparation:—
Canada, Vancouver Island, Saskatchewan, The Fraser Valley, The Okanagan Valley, Winnipeg.

Printed and bound by
D. W. Friesen & Sons Ltd.,
Altona, Manitoba, Canada.

DUNCAN McDOUGALL F.R.P.S.

Duncan McDougall was born in Scotland, and came to Canada in 1952. After living in the Toronto area for seven years, where he studied photography at Ryerson College, he moved to the Yukon to photograph the rugged splendour of the Canadian North. Three years later Duncan travelled south to Vancouver where he lives today with his wife and two children.

As well as photography, Duncan is interested in music, travel, and mountain climbing. In 1967, he was selected to be a member of the Yukon Alpine Centennial Expedition, a group organized to climb previously unconquered peaks in the St. Elias range of Kluane National Park, in the Yukon Territory.

Now established as one of North America's leading photographers, Duncan is currently photographing Canada for a new book to be published in the fall of 1980. He was elected to the fellowship of the Royal Photographic Society in 1970.

There are three books by Duncan McDougall in this series. The other two are 'Victoria' and 'Toronto'.

Contents

Introduction

The story of this city begins in 1792 with the voyage of Captain George Vancouver who, like many before him, came in search of the Northwest Passage. He was not new to the Pacific Northwest region. As a midshipman, along with another junior officer, the notorious William Bligh, he had been part of Captain James Cook's expedition which explored Nootka Sound on the west coast of Vancouver Island. This was in 1778, the year before Cook met his fate at the hands of the natives of the Sandwich Islands.

Although Cook's expedition did not land on the mainland, the landing on Vancouver Island constituted the first European contact with the west coast of Canada. George Vancouver returned in 1792 as captain of his own expedition. He mapped and surveyed the area that is now downtown Vancouver. Giving appropriate British names to many of the geographical features he returned home, little imagining that in less than one hundred years his name would be immortalized in this timber covered wilderness.

Sixteen years later, the intrepid explorer Simon Fraser following the course of the river that today bears his name, arrived in what is now Marpole. Stopping, he turned back in disgust; knowing that this could not be the mouth of the Columbia River which he had believed he was travelling.

For approximately the next sixty years the western part of the Burrard inlet lay in limbo. Other than a few sporadic incursions the area was largely ignored. Settlement concentrated to the east in New Westminster, and Fort Langley until the mid eighteen sixties when the inexorable thrust westward continued. Granville Townsite developed in the area that today is Gastown. Both figuratively, and literally Gastown is a monument to its founder "Gassy" Jack Deighton; the spiritual father of Vancouver after whom Gastown was named.

Jack Deighton came to Granville from New Westminster in 1867 to set up a saloon and slake the thirsts of the workers in the area. Today the street numbering system in Vancouver starts at the site of his saloon, on the corner of Carrall and Water streets. It is a tribute to the effective job he did, and to the lasting impression he made on the growing community.

Despite the gradual expansion of the township, Granville was little more than an appendage to New Westminster and seemed destined to slip into obscurity. With the coming of the railroad, however, Granville's destiny was changed irrevocably. In April of 1886 Granville was incorporated as the city of Vancouver and almost immediately — in June of the same year — was razed by fire. It seems almost a tradition that all great cities must have their fire to set them on the road to greatness, and Vancouver was no exception. Undaunted, the city fathers set up their city hall in a tent and went about the business of rebuilding. In the process, they set aside for the public use the land that is today Stanley Park; an inspired move for which Vancouverites and visitors alike are ever grateful.

In May of 1887 the railroad finally arrived in Vancouver bringing a boom of expansion. Shipping increased to connect with the railroad making the city Canada's main west coast seaport. Hotels, houses, industry and bridges sprang up and the mood of expansion has continued with normal peaks and valleys to the present time. The railroad brought with it the most precious commodity of all — immigrants. Mostly of British stock, they gave the young city the distinctive British stamp which it has retained over the years.

Vancouver is less than one hundred years old. An infant among the cities of the world. Yet, in little more than the space of one lifetime, men of vision; ambitious, determined men have wrenched the land from the forest and built the metropolis that is today's Vancouver. The Vancouver presented in this book is the Vancouver of enchanting parks, tall buildings, and the modern harbour. All stand as a monument to the pioneer spirit which expanded Canada "From sea to sea" and in the process gave us this city.

(Preceding page:) Looking towards the North Shore from the top of the Sheraton-Landmark Hotel.

(Opposite:) The Hotel Vancouver. The present building was completed in 1939, and replaced an older structure built in 1916.

(Left:) The rose garden in Stanley Park.

(Below:) English Bay Beach. The beach is a popular spot for visitors and downtown residents throughout the year.

(Preceding two pages:) Vancouver by night.

(Right:) A tugboat manoeuvring a container ship into place.

(Below:) The Marine Building.

(Opposite right:) Paddle wheelers docked near the entrance to Stanley Park.

(Opposite below:) A Barrow's Goldeneye duck resting on the rudder of a vessel.

(Preceding pages:) Pleasure craft in the False Creek Marina. In the background are the mountains on the North Shore and the skyscraper offices of downtown Vancouver.

(Opposite:) The West Coast Transmission building; one of the most uniquely designed buildings in Vancouver.

(Left:) The Sears Tower with its revolving restaurant.

(Below:) Evening sun on ships anchored in English Bay.

(Right:) The Bloedel Conservatory on Little Mountain in Queen Elizabeth Park.

(Below:) The gardens in Queen Elizabeth Park. This site was originally a quarry.

(Opposite:) The Orpheum Theatre, home of the Vancouver Symphony Orchestra.

(Opposite:) The Robson Square complex. Completed in 1978 the square houses the Vancouver Law Courts, provincial offices, and has various exhibitions, displays, and public functions throughout the year.

(Left:) The stainless steel sculpture at the entrance to the Planetarium by George Norris.

(Below:) The Planetarium.

(Following page:) English Bay sunset.

The City of Vancouver

There are few among us who can resist the lure of the west. The pursuit of the setting sun in search of some mystical Shangri-La is an impulse as old as mankind. For those countless numbers of Canadians and other nationalities who have trekked west to stay or visit, Vancouver is that Shangri-La.

The attraction is at once physical and ethereal. It is as much the awe derived from the sheer beauty of its natural setting, as it is the expression of Canadian western movement over the past two centuries. If the railroad was the national dream, Vancouver represents the fulfillment of that dream. It is as much the climate, tempered by the Coast range mountains, as the fact that Vancouver is the most immediate link Canadians have with their brief history. The history of Canada is short; Vancouver reflects that history in microcosm.

Most Canadian cities have some glowing adjective bestowed upon them by the inhabitants. Montreal is cosmopolitan, and Toronto sophisticated. By contrast Vancouverites are serenely confident. Serene in the knowledge that here lies the good life, they feel no compelling urge to shout the city's virtues from the rooftops. When one visits Canada's third largest city it is easy to realize why this attitude exists.

When King George VI, and Queen Elizabeth visited Vancouver in 1939, Her Majesty was heard to remark: "This seems to me the place to live." Since then over one million people have paid tribute to her statement.

Vancouver is indeed synonymous with the good life. Few other cities have such a diversity of life styles to offer. The pace is your choice. There is truly something for everyone. As either participant or spectator, one can enjoy a simple nature ramble through Stanley Park, a rigorous hike in the wilderness or a quiet cup of tea at English Bay as you watch the freighters waiting to discharge their cargo. Because of the balmy climate, the snow generally stays where it belongs — on the mountains. It is possible in mid-winter to golf in the morning, or afternoon, and ski the same day on one of the three fine ski slopes that surround the city. This experience is unique to Vancouver and is savoured to its fullest extent by the residents.

(Right:) The statue of "Gassy" Jack Deighton, and the hotel Europe. Familiar landmarks of Gastown.

(Below:) Chinatown's Pender street by night. Vancouver has the second largest oriental population in any North American city.

(Opposite right:) Harbour scene in the Burrard inlet. The Sea-Bus can be seen en route to the North Shore.

(Opposite below:) The Port of Vancouver with the City of North Vancouver in the background.

The nostalgia enthusiast is by no means disappointed in Vancouver. At Kitsilano Beach stands the symbol of the iron band that welded this country together: Engine 374, which brought the first passenger train from Montreal into Vancouver. A short distance away the maritime museum houses the RCMP vessel St. Roch. This was the first ship to sail the Northwest Passage in both directions. The seafaring history of Vancouver and British Columbia is represented in a variety of exhibits in the Maritime Museum. The museum was Vancouver's B.C. centennial project. For those people whose interest lie with the land the Centennial Museum carries displays of early pioneer days dress and equipment, together with some stimulating scenes of early native culture.

No description of Vancouver would be complete if the reader were left with the impression that Stanley Park is the only park of consequence in the city.

There are many other fine parks and gardens that are to be enjoyed at various points throughout the city. Queen Elizabeth Park, situated atop Little Mountain, virtually in the geographical centre of the city, was once a rock quarry. Today, with a spectacular view of the city and its environs on four sides the park is a paradise of beauty. The dominant feature of this park is the Bloedel Floral conservatory, a huge plexiglass dome housing over three hundred species of tropical florae. Once inside the dome, one may expect to be serenaded by a choir of equally exotic tropical song birds who are allowed to fly freely within the serenity of this verdant refuge. The sunken gardens, the walks and most of all the view, make this a photographer's paradise.

Formerly a golf course, Van Dusen Botanical Gardens, situated on Oak Street about the mid point between downtown and the Fraser River has a host of exciting and interesting displays to offer not only the serious horticulturist, but the curious visitor too. Opened in 1975, the garden covers 55½ rolling acres, contains seven small lakes and over 3300 different species of plant life. The construction of this garden is quite naturally an ongoing process, thus it is impossible to predict the final tally. With a variety of greenhouses strategically located, flowers, plants and herbs from all over the world provide a scintillating display. Highlights are the Children's Garden, Fragrance garden and Herbal garden. In the amphitheatre, films on forest succession and maintenance can be seen and the MacMillan-Bloedel audio-visual "Walk in the Forest" is a stroll with a difference. Sculptures from the Symposium of 1975 have been erected at various points throughout the park, adding a total effect of rich diversity.

John Hendry Park (swimming and fishing in Trout Lake), China Creek Park (bicycle racing), University Endowment Lands and Marine Drive Foreshore Park (horse riding) are but another few of many parks to be enjoyed within the city limits and which contribute so richly to Vancouver's life-style.

In Vancouver's East End overlooking the Burrard Inlet is Exhibition Park. Here set in 172 acres of land is the site of the Pacific National Exhibition. Held every summer for 17 days this exhibition provides a forum for the achievements and interests of the people of British Columbia. It is the fifth largest event of its kind in North America.

Throughout the year the park hosts many agricultural, trade, and commercial exhibitions. Shows for the Home and Garden, Boat, and Automobile are but a few which attract many people from Vancouver, and the Lower Mainland.

Here too, is the pulse of the city's professional sports scene, and the site of British Columbia's Sports Hall of Fame. At Empire Stadium, built for the 1954 Commonwealth Games, the B.C. Lions of the Canadian Football League play between August and November.

During the summer, Empire Stadium is home to Vancouver's most popular sports team — the Vancouver Whitecaps of the North American Soccer League. In 1979 the Whitecaps won the N.A.S.L. 'Soccer Bowl'.

At the eastern border of the park lies the Pacific Coliseum, and during the National Hockey League season the Coliseum is "home ice" for the Vancouver Canucks hockey team. The building seats over 16,000 spectators, and is used for many other attractions.

For those who wish to be part of the action wagers may be made at the Exhibition Park race track. Here thoroughbred horses race around the five furlong track.

The future of Vancouver seems exciting, and as the city approaches its first century of existence the people of Vancouver are confident of their city and life-style for the next century.

The Sears Tower with the North Shore in the background

Stainless steel creation at the Pacific Centre at Georgia and Granville Streets.

The North Shore

Across the Burrard Inlet and at either end, stand two massive bridges, linking the City of Vancouver to the North Shore. At the west end, guarding the entrance to the natural harbour stands the First Narrows or Lions Gate Bridge. To the east is the Second Narrows Bridge. Together these structures form an iron bracket around the busy waters of the inlet carrying a constant stream of traffic to and from the North Shore; or "North Van" and "West Van" as the municipalities are known locally.

One of the most spectacular drives in the world is through the tree-lined avenue of Stanley Park, on to the Lions Gate Bridge and an exhilarating view of the Port of Vancouver. To take this drive is to have the feeling of being shot from a cannon out of the permanent twilight of the trees into the bright panorama ahead. On the other side of the bridge awaits the North Shore.

Among most urban dwellers there is a tendency to think of the suburbs as merely bedroom communities, but North Shore citizens would protest this label most vigorously. The North Shore and the communities of North Vancouver and West Vancouver have as much a claim to the history and beauty of the area as does Greater Vancouver. While an integral part of the landscape, North Vancouver is yet another community grown from the humble beginnings of a logging camp. Its growth story closely parallels that of the city on the south shore.

In 1863 Pioneer Mill was established at what is today the bottom of Lonsdale Street in North Vancouver. After a couple of owners were unable to keep their heads above water, the mill came into the hands of one Sewell Moody. The Mill became known as Moody's Mill, among other more loose terms.

The group of shacks which sprang up around the area became known quite naturally as Moodyville. At first Moody appeared to be plagued by the same problems running the mill as the previous owners.

Luck was on his side however. Road expansion to and from New Westminster together, with the influx of more and more settlers ensured the eventual success of his operation. Blessed as it was with a natural deep water port and acres and acres of virgin forest to work with. Unfortunately Moody did not live to see the fruits of his labours in the great development of the North Shore. On November 4, 1775 while en route from Victoria to San Francisco, the S.S. Pacific on which Moody was a passenger struck another vessel and was lost with all but two of her passengers drowning.

Incorporated as the District of North Vancouver in 1891, the North Shore has never looked back. Today it is a vibrant residential community with fine modern shipyards and port facilities.

Spectacular is the word required to describe the topography of the North Shore. Clinging to the slopes of the North Shore mountains the residential area of British Properties and a variety of other communities enjoy a view over downtown Vancouver, the Burrard Inlet, the Georgia Strait and on a clear day even Vancouver Island. A stimulating existence indeed.

To the west, the burgeoning community of West Vancouver originally a summer cottage resort, grew with the building of the Lions Gate Bridge, and now stretches its way around the point towards the highway north to Horseshoe Bay and Squamish.

From east to west, Seymour, Grouse and Hollyburn mountains are the dominant features on the skyline: with the "Twins" or the "Lions" standing as silent sentinel over the whole stunning array.

Mount Seymour, reached by the Second Narrows Bridge is a Provincial Park which offers excellent skiing in the winter and many well marked hiking trails to be enjoyed in the warmer months. A modern highway runs to approximately the 3000 foot level, weaving its way through switchback after switchback to the ski centre near the summit.

Grouse Mountain, perhaps the most spectacular of all three, soars almost 4000 feet straight up. The trip to the summit of this peak is one of the most exhilarating in the land.

The Grouse Mountain Skyride is a full five minute trip in a gondola car covering a mile in distance at heights of up to two hundred feet above the ground, following a path up the slope to the Grouse Nest Chalet at the 3700 foot level. From here the view is absolutely breathtaking, particularly at night when the lights of the lower mainland and even the lights of Northern Washington State can be seen quite clearly. Again, as on Seymour, skiing and hiking is available to those enthusiasts in their particular season.

Another skiing or hiking area is Hollyburn Mountain a few miles to the west. Cypress Bowl, one of the newest ski facilities on the local scene is part of this beautiful park which has an alpine setting and is fast becoming one of the more popular resort areas of the Vancouver locale.

Yet there is more than mountain terrain to the North Shore. For a truly heart-stopping experience, a visit to the Capilano Canyon suspension bridge is a must for the visitor. Built in 1899 this 450 foot footbridge hangs over two hundred feet above the Capilano River. It is only the strongest of strong hearts that can fail to skip a beat as one snakes and sways across the river during an exciting yet totally safe trip.

Lynn Canyon park while perhaps not quite as spectacular as Capilano provides a refreshing alternative to the hustle and bustle of its more tourist oriented neighbour. With its murmuring waterfalls and serene walks through evergreen glades this park gives one some idea of how the whole area appeared to the first white settlers a little over one hundred years ago.

Indeed the North Shore is singularly blessed with natural parks. During a short ten minute flight from the Port of Vancouver over North and West Vancouver one is immediately impressed with the quantity of green below. It is a compliment to the planners of the area that while interested in the residential and business development prospects of the community, over the years they have maintained a healthy balance with nature whilst keeping a stern eye on the ecology.

(Preceding pages:) The downtown Vancouver skyline from False Creek. (Above right:) Mixed flower garden in Stanley park. (Below right:) A popcorn vendor along English Bay. (Right above:)

(Preceding two pages:) An autumn scene near Beaver Lake in Stanley Park.

(Right:) The Stanley Park Pavillion.

(Below:) Polar bears in the Stanley Park Zoo.

(Opposite:) Lost Lagoon.

(Right:) A King penguin in Stanley Park Zoo.

(Below:) A Killer whale in the Vancouver Aquarium.

(Opposite:) Fall in Stanley Park.

(Following two pages:) Sunset from second beach.

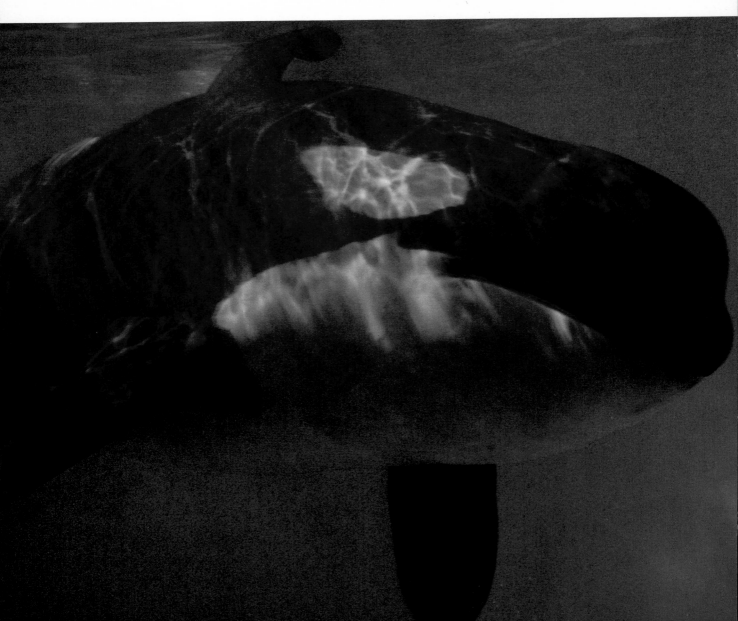

(Opposite:) Lighthouse Park in West Vancouver.

(Left:) Boats moored near the West Vancouver Marina.

(Below:) The Horseshoe Bay ferry terminal. From here travellers depart to Vancouver Island, and the Sunshine Coast.

(Right:) The Grouse Mountain Skyride, one of the more popular attractions in Vancouver. The cable cars whisk sightseers and skiers to the top where the view is spectacular.

(Below:) Capilano Lake, with the "Lions" in the background.

(Opposite:) Skiers on Grouse Mountain.

(Opposite:) The Capilano River as it leaves the canyon. Every fall thousands of salmon return here to make their final journey to spawn at the Capilano Hatchery upstream.

(Left:) Capilano Canyon as viewed from the Cleveland Dam in North Vancouver.

(Below:) The serenity of Deep Cove.

(Following page:) A scene in Lynn Valley Park.

Richmond

To the south of the city of Vancouver across the north arm of the Fraser River are the municipalities of Richmond, and Delta. These two areas also encompass the communities of Steveston, Ladner, and Tsawwassen.

A late development on the Vancouver and district scene, Richmond has become one of the fastest growing urban communities in the lower mainland. Yet despite the speed of its commercial, and residential growth Richmond is very conscious of its history. In Minoru Park, the Chapel in the Park, originally built in 1891 and lately restored is a fine example of an early pioneer house of worship. For enthusiasts of military, and aeronautical history the nearby museum has displays on these subjects along with appropriate items of local interest. A well supplied art gallery is also part of this interesting complex.

Richmond is the site of the Vancouver International Airport. The airport is the third busiest civil airport in Canada, accommodating one aircraft movement every three minutes. An eight mile drive from downtown Vancouver, the airport is situated on Sea Island between the north, and middle arms of the Fraser River. The commercial air services operating from Vancouver International are provided by domestic air carriers to points within British Columbia, and the rest of Canada. Domestic and foreign airlines connect Vancouver with the western United States, Mexico, South America, Europe, Australia, Japan, and other Pacific destinations. All Canadian air traffic to and from the Pacific Rim area connect through Vancouver International, and the majority of British Columbia cities depend on Vancouver International for flight connections to the rest of Canada. All told the airport will handle 7½ million people in the course of one year.

(Opposite Above:) Vegetable farming in the Fraser River delta.

(Opposite below:) Along River Road.

(Left:) Vancouver International Airport.

(Below:) A secluded corner of Steveston.

(Right:) A Great Blue Heron along River Road.

(Below:) Sunrise on the Fraser River.

(Opposite page:) Part of British Columbia's fishing fleet.

Burnaby

Originally a tract of bush and wasteland sandwiched between the City of New Westminster and the growing community of Granville, the Municipality of Burnaby is today the only suburb of Greater Vancouver not separated from the main city by some physical boundary. Indeed only the changed colour of the street signs on most avenues advises the traveller he has left the one and entered the other. This is by no means to denigrate the suburb, for despite this apparent fusion the citizens of Burnaby consider themselves a race apart and indeed make an essential contribution to the life-style of both their own municipality and to the Vancouver area in general.

It appears that there was some possible settlement in the Deer Lake area of Burnaby as far back as 1860. It was not however until the 1890s that any serious attempt was made to settle or build. At that time, several enterprising gentlemen from the New Westminster area recognized the commercial and residential possibilities of the area. Strategically placed between the two major communities, they established themselves and ultimately petitioned the provincial capital in Victoria to approve their new community as a township. It was to be called Burnaby, after the erstwhile secretary of Colonel Moody. The petition was approved immediately, and Burnaby was on its way.

The wisdom of these gentlemen was well-founded, and if they were able today to view the fruits of their ideas, one has the feeling one would get a resounding "I told you so" from them.

For, as the burgeoning port city of Vancouver grew, the expanding work force required much additional living space. Much of this would be provided in Burnaby.

As in the general area, most of the bush and wilderness has disappeared. Today Burnaby is a modern sophisticated municipality in its own right, yet like its neighbours the citizens of Burnaby have protected much of their heritage while looking towards future development.

For their B.C. Centennial project, the people of Burnaby constructed Heritage Village. Here, western village life at the turn of the century is recreated in a "living museum". Here one may watch the village blacksmith at work, watch the local newspaper come to life and study examples of the leisure life of the folk of those bygone days. By the side of Deer Lake in Century Gardens a variety of stores in the decor of the times gives one a realistic idea of life in early Burnaby.

To the delight of the citizens of Burnaby, they have something that Vancouver does not have. An actual mountain. (Little Mountain in Vancouver is rather an ambitious title for what is not really much more than a large hill.) Quite naturally, called Burnaby Mountain, this peak commands a panoramic view of the surrounding area, including Indian Arm Inlet, Delta, the City of Vancouver and Vancouver Island. Here again is a peaceful retreat from the more practical activities of the city streets below.

Atop Burnaby Mountain is Simon Fraser Univeristy. The modern buildings will eventually accommodate up to 12,000 students. This masterpiece of academic construction was the work of several local architects, most notably Arthur Erickson and Geoffrey Massey. Opened in September 1965, the building designs and architecture have won many awards.

On the boundary between Vancouver, Central Park provides another haven for the weary. Set in 100 acres of forest, one has some idea of the odds that faced the original settlers of this area as they attempted to clear land for living space without the modern heavy equipment we know today. Swangard Stadium, part of this complex is the scene of many fine international rugby encounters, with teams from all over the world competing against British Columbia's best.

(Following pages:) Central Park in Burnaby.

New Westminster

In 1827 the Hudson's Bay Company whose history is so inexorably linked to that of Canada, responding to the relentless pressure of increasing American expansion in Washington and Oregon established Fort Langley, thirty miles upstream on the Fraser River. This was to be the first of a series of trading posts and sixteen years later the same company established Fort Camosun to become Fort Victoria, and then Victoria. The Oregon Treaty of 1846 assigned the whole of Vancouver Island to Britain under the control of the Company, and in 1849 the Island was made a British crown colony. The Company, jealously guarding its fur trade had no intention of introducing settlers into either the new colony or the lower mainland since this would destroy their source of furs. As far as the Company was concerned then, Fort Victoria and Fort Langley were destined for quiet and peaceful obscurity on the furthest reaches of the Empire.

By 1858 the California gold rush of '49 was to all intents and purposes over. Those lucky ones who had made their fortunes, and luckier still perhaps who kept them stayed in California. Those not so fortunate sought new claims to dig, and in 1858 the cry of "Gold" went up along the Fraser River — the rush was on. Almost overnight, 25,000 men flocked to the lower mainland and the planned quite and peaceful obscurity of Forts Langley and Victoria were shattered forever. That year the crown colony of British Columbia was founded on the mainland with James Douglas as its governor and in 1859 the city of New Westminster was established as the capital of that colony. Given its name by Queen Victoria, the first city of British Columbia took on the appendage the Royal City, a title it has carried proudly up to the present time.

In 1866 the two colonies of Vancouver Island and British Columbia united under the name of the latter and adopted the growing New Westminster as capital of the new enlarged colony. The citizens of this first and capital city of British Columbia looked forward dreamily to a future of grandeur, glory and prosperity. Alas these dreams were to be ambushed by a harsh reality.

The residents of Vancouver Island, the first colony and the citizens of Victoria, the first capital, had consistently pressed their claim that their city had a prior claim to the title of capital. Consequently in 1868 after months of political infighting, and back-room wrangling, the capital was transferred from New Westminster to Victoria. Quite naturally to the delight of Victoria but to the chagrin of New Westminster. It is said rather caustically that those in New Westminster who screamed the loudest in protest against the proposed move, were among the first to move to Victoria along with the governor, his retinue and the host of civil servants. Most notable among these deserters was John Robson the fiery editor of the British Columbian newspaper who immediately transferred his belongings lock, stock and barrel across the strait and set up another newspaper in the new capital.

Despite this adversity and the economic problems caused by the reversal of fortunes, New Westminster continued to prosper and continued to hurl defiance at the bogus capital across the water. A tradition that is maintained to the present time, though with perhaps a less vehement tone than at the outset. Still, there are citizens of New Westminster who will tell you today that their city is the true capital of the province and if it is not the physical capital, it is certainly the spiritual one.

In the 1850s the Royal Engineers arrived in New Westminster to maintain peace and order in the district, and left an indelible mark on the city. The district of Sapperton takes its name from the "sappers" who were responsible for most of the early construction on the steep slopes rising above the Fraser River. Still standing today is the Irving House Historical centre, originally the home of Captain William Irving, a steamboat operator. Built by the Royal Engineers and designed by T. C. Graham, the original owner of Moody's Mill on the North Shore, it is now a museum containing many fine artifacts detailing the developing life of the community. The house itself is a splendid example of the period architecture and contains much of the original furnishings brought over from Britain at the time of its building.

Time and progress have changed the face of New Westminster over the years. Yet like the rest of the residents of the west coast they have not completely turned their back on their British origins.

New Westminster is home to the Salmonbellies of lacrosse fame. It is fitting therefore that Canada's true national sport should be celebrated in British Columbia's first city in the Lacrosse Hall of Fame.

Today more industrial and residential than at any point in their history, the citizens still find time each year to celebrate a four-day May festival in the old English tradition, during which one of the local beauties is crowned May Queen. And, out of respect and gratitude to the grand dame who gave the city its name, a twenty-one gun salute is fired on Queen Victoria's birthday each year. It is just possible she might be amused!

(Right:) Tugboats in New Westminster. Although some miles from the open sea New Westminster is a major west coast port handling vessels from around the world.

(Below:) Fog under the Patullo Bridge in New Westminster.

(Opposite:) Symbols of the fishing industry.